DOUBLE ACT

IAN HENERY & DAVID MOORE

Double Act

Ian Henery & David Moore

ISBN-13: 978-1-912605-84-2

ISBN-10: 1-912605-84-8

Text © 2023 Ian Henery & David Moore

Photographs © 2023 David Moore

Published in Great Britain by j-views Publishing, 2025

Cover art © 2025 David Moore

All rights reserved. No part of this publication may be reproduced, stored in a retrieval system or transmitted, in any form or by any means, without the prior permission of both the copyright holder and the publisher in writing.

j-views Publishing, 26 Lombard St, Lichfield, WS13 6DR   publish@j-views.biz   www.j-views.biz

Double Act

These photographs and writing comprised part of an exhibition held at the Library of Birmingham in the first half of 2025.

Entitled *In Search of Urban Happiness*, the exhibition was paralleled by a similar exhibition in Halifax.

David Moore, a social historian, wrote words and took photographs to illustrate his perception of Birmingham landmarks

Further illustrations in poetic form were provided by Ian Henery, a well-known award-winning local poet and radio presenter.

Together, these words and images provide haunting personal interpretations of many of Birmingham's major features, ranging from the famous central Bull of the Bullring to housing estates on the edges of the city.

CONTENTS

Double Act...iii
Foreword by Dave Allen, The Grid Project......................................vi
Foreword by Dr Dorian Chan...vii
Book Review by Dee and Keith Hirst...vii
Preface by David Moore..viii

LANDMARKS

Spaghetti Junction..2
Gravelly Hill Interchange, Junction 6 of the M6 (haiku).......................3
Birmingham Spaghetti Western..3
Lord Nelson Monument..4
Because There Is No C In Birmingham (acrostic)................................5
Conversation with Horatio Nelson in Birmingham's Bullring.....................5
Edgbaston Cricket Ground..7
Edgbaston Cricket Ground (haiku)..8
Holy Trinity Church...9
Holy Trinity Church, Camphill (haiku)..10
Birthplace of Birmingham City Football Club..................................10

EDGES

Moseley Golf Course..12
Moseley Golf Course (haiku)..12
Moseley Golf Club..13

NODES

Birmingham Bullring..16
Bull in the Bullring (villanelle)..17
Released from the Shackles of Oppression (Bull in the Bullring)..............18

DISTRICTS

Short Heath – New Utopia. 20
Post World War One Idealism – A Municipal Dream 21
Sonnet To Slightly Bruised Fruit. 21
The Little Path. 22
Suburban Dawn (After Brendan Hawthorne's "Urban Dawn"). 22
The Lisieux Trust in Marsh Lane (villanelle)(NeurodiVERSE) 23
Court Farm Primary School (rondeau) ("Dream, Believe, Achieve"). 24
Conversation In A Pub (Apologies to Tom Waits and the 1973 album *Closing Time*) 24
Remains of Tram Lines on a Central Reservation 25
Thick as a Brick (Apologies to Jethro Tull and the 1972 album *Thick as a Brick*) 26
Short Heath Graffiti (one last time) 26

PATHS

Moseley Road - a Journey from Victorian Inequality to a Wealth of Cultural Diversity. 28
Moseley Road (found poem) (Apologies to Ocean Colour Scene) 30
The Old House (Ferndale House, Moseley Road) 30
Thumbs Up To A Road Sweeper On Moseley Road 30
Night on Moseley Road Waiting For The Foodbank To Open (Quakers Friends' Institute). 31
A Cup of Tea At The Foodbank (Quakers Friends' Institute). 32
The Khanda on Moseley Road 33
Balsall Heath Library & Moseley Road Baths 33

Foreword by Dave Allen, The Grid Project

Double Act has its roots in the collaborative photography venture *In Search of Urban Happiness*, run in 2023 by The Grid Project. David Moore and Ian Henery were participants in that project, along with 43 other contributors: in total, 3631 photographs and 262 written pieces were produced. What you see in this book are the poems that Ian wrote and the photographs that David made as their contributions.

It's appropriate, then, to give a bit of background about The Grid Project. It's a project I have run for over 20 years and is concerned with perceptions of our urban environments: this is its only agenda.

Initially, in 2002, The Grid Project was a bit of a backlash, a backlash against the picturesque, slick, pretty – even touristy photographs of urban environments. In order to challenge participant photographers to describe the urban environment in different ways we experimented with the grids we find on maps. Wherever an intersection occurred, that became the location for a photograph, whatever may have been found at that location. We developed a mission statement.

> A photographic grid is a collaborative venture which aims to make a meaningful visual statement about an environment by adopting a systematic approach. What does this place look like? What does this place feel like? The grid imposes a system that may sometimes locate the picturesque but is just as likely to find the industrial, the rugged, the new, old, boring, threatening or just ugly.

Who is the 'we' developing these ideas? I'm a fine artist by training and have spent my career teaching art, graphics, photography and art history. My initial collaborator when developing the first few projects was Professor Jerry Tew at The University of Birmingham.

The 2002 project was exhibited in 2003 in The Dean Clough Galleries in Halifax. By 2007 the ideas had crystallised sufficiently to take on Birmingham. Except that we couldn't quite take on Birmingham – it's too big. At the time we would exhibit the photographs in a grid that matched the maps we were working from. To do this for the whole of Birmingham would have resulted in a grid of photographs so small that their content would be lost. We needed to tighten our focus and did this by using the outer circle bus route as our boundary. Apart from its convenient size, it also *means* something to Brummies. *Inside The Outer Circle* became our first big exhibition in Birmingham, on display on a huge wall in The Mailbox throughout 2008.

Since then, the total number of exhibitions is 14, including shows in The Dean Clough Galleries, Halifax, The Yorkshire Sculpture Park, Tate Liverpool, The Herbert Gallery, Coventry, The Warwick Arts Centre and Birmingham Central Library.

Although most of the projects have involved some kind of map-based variation of the original idea, other approaches have been used. Here's a couple.

Phyllis Nicklin's work was uncovered in 2015, having slept in a filing cabinet for a *long* time. Her photographs of Birmingham generated emotional responses and raised the eyebrows of most of the photography fraternity. She is a Brummie hero. So, in 2017, rather than repeat the map-based project of 2007 a decade on, we decided to pay homage to Nicklin by revisiting the sites she had photographed between 1957 and 1969. *In The Footsteps of Phyllis...*

And then there's this, the most recent project – *In search of Urban Happiness* (2023). Still concerned with the urban environment, it is based on *The Image of the City* (1960) by Kevin Lynch. This book, the result of a 5-year study, introduced the concept of 'imageability' or the quality that makes a place distinct and memorable. Lynch identified five key features affecting a city's imageability: paths, districts, landmarks, edges and nodes. We used these features on this project as the subjects for our photographs and writing. You'll see Ian Henery and David Moore's responses on the pages that follow.

Dave Allen
The Grid Project
October 2025

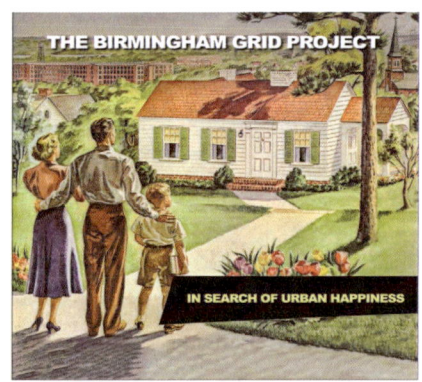

Foreword by Dr Dorian Chan

As the Secretary General of the Birmingham Chinatown Business Association, it is my honour to contribute to this remarkable collection of poetry and prose, *Double Act* from David Moore & Ian Henery. This book is a celebration of Birmingham's rich history, its vibrant communities, and the enduring spirit of its people. Through the lens of two talented writers, David Moore and Ian Henery, we are invited to explore the city's landmarks, districts, and cultural nodes, each brought to life with vivid imagery and heartfelt emotion.

Birmingham is a city of contrasts and connections—a place where the past and present co-exist, where industrial heritage meets modern innovation, and where diverse communities come together to create a tapestry of shared experiences. This book captures that essence beautifully, weaving together stories of resilience, transformation, and hope. From the social housing ideals of Short Heath to the iconic Spaghetti Junction, from the historic Moseley Road to the bustling Bullring, the authors take us on a journey that is both deeply personal and universally resonant.

As someone who has witnessed the dynamism of Birmingham's Chinatown and its role in shaping the city's identity, I am particularly moved by the themes of inclusion and diversity that run through this work. The poems and essays remind us of the importance of community, the power of cultural heritage, and the need to honour the contributions of all who call Birmingham home.

This book is not just a tribute to Birmingham's landmarks and history; it is a call to reflect on the values that unite us and the dreams that inspire us. It is a testament to the creativity and passion of its authors, and a gift to all who cherish the spirit of this great city.

I commend David Moore and Ian Henery for their outstanding work and invite readers to immerse themselves in the pages that follow. May this book inspire you to see Birmingham—and the world around you—with fresh eyes and a renewed sense of wonder.

Sincerely,

Dr. Dorian Chan
Secretary General
Birmingham Chinatown Business Association

Book Review by Dee and Keith Hirst

Dee works with (Creative Art Showcase – Charity), and husband Keith Hirst CBE is former Chief Executive of Metsec PLC

With both of us having strong connections into industry in Birmingham and the Black Country it was touching to see the combined photographs by David Moore and Ian Henery creating a snapshot of diversity, in the beating heart of Birmingham.

The creative life of Britain's second city needed to be showcased and put on a public platform for all to see and enjoy and this book really does it. If you have ever worked in this city this book will remind you in an elegant and inclusive way of the people and places, we all know.

Beg, steal or borrow this book – you'll love it. Or why not invest in it for you and your reception area to share the love!

Dee & Keith Hirst

Preface by David Moore

I have lived and worked in Birmingham for most of my life. It is the place I love; it is my home.

I am a child of the reconciliation generation following WWII—a time when a sense of community built a foundation of support for family, friends, and neighbours.

Over my lifetime, Birmingham has seen significant change: widespread bombing in WWII leaving vast areas of dereliction, followed by several major redevelopments of the city centre and growth in the industrial sector. This growth led to calls for more labour to work in this industrial heartland, a need that could only be met by welcoming immigrants. The people of Ireland came and built our infrastructure. The Windrush generation came and worked on buses and in the big manufacturing plants—ICI, Dunlop, and the GEC, to name but a few.

I feel privileged to have grown up in this environment. Despite a poor education, I was able to live in, learn from, and enjoy this diverse environment and its community.

This book is the result of a lifelong conversation. It is a personal love letter to a city and its people, who have been part of relentless change and enduring spirit, created in a time when, to me, celebrating what we have in common, what we share together, and how we care for each other—the things that bring us together—feels more important than ever.

The project you hold in your hands began with the ideas of Kevin Lynch, who taught us that a 'legible city'—one with clear paths, landmarks, and nodes—gives its residents a profound sense of emotional security. We used his framework not as a rigid academic exercise, but as a lens to focus on the real, living Birmingham.

I ventured out to capture these elements—the paths of Moseley Road, the nodes of the Bullring, the edges of Spaghetti Junction—not just as physical spaces, but as vessels of memory, meaning, and emotional potency.

While out photographing, I worked alone, but this was never a solitary journey. The heart of this project is collaboration. My photographs and narratives are in a constant, joyful dialogue with the superb poetry of Ian Henery. This 'double act' mirrors the collaborative spirit of the city itself.

I spent time with several people on my travels: the people working in the food bank, the street cleaner, and the shopkeeper. All of whom I had interesting dialogues with; each one was an opportunity to learn and reflect. We would part with a handshake, both of us enriched by the chance encounter.

As I documented the city, a central theme emerged with undeniable force: Birmingham's greatest landmark is not a building or a road, but its cultural richness. From the gilded inequalities of the Victorian era to the vibrant, super-diverse communities of today, the city's story is one of continuous transformation. We see this in the Guru Nanak Gurdwara standing proud, in the Quakers' Institute reborn as a food bank, and in the bull of the Bullring, transformed from a symbol of baiting to one of strength and community.

In the face of divisive political rhetoric, this book is a quiet but firm testament to a different truth. Birmingham is a cultural integration success story. It is a place where civility and conviviality are built into the very fabric of our streets, a place where a 'Wealth of Cultural Diversity' is our greatest asset.

So, as you turn these pages, I invite you to see Birmingham through our eyes. See the resilience in its old stones and the hope in its new faces. We hope you will find, as we have, that the city's true imageability lies in its people and their shared, ongoing project of building a community for all. Thank you for joining us on this journey.

LANDMARKS

Spaghetti Junction

The construction of spaghetti junction swept away a significant chunk of Gravelly Hill and Aston under a promise of a better life for all. A modern Birmingham for a modern age. I was sold on the idea. I like building sites and the technology and machinery used in the construction matched all of my expectations and the promises of the planners. It was indeed a mammoth construction and engineering endeavour that we had not seen on this scale before in Birmingham.

The name Spaghetti Junction was soon coined and looking at the plans you could see why. I was so excited and watched its construction progress on a daily basis. I went in all the parts of that construction site where we should not have gone.

The area around Salford Bridge was quite a vibrant community with rows of shops extending around Slade Road and the Erdington Arms pub on the corner. Leamington Road, Bridge Road, Woodland Road and the bottom half of Copeley Hill were row after row of terraced houses. The top half of Copeley Hill had half a dozen very large, detached houses with Burlington House at the top. It was used as a Reform School; the neglected gardens still had a derelict swimming pool.

Underneath the intended Spaghetti junction were the meeting points of the river Tame's confluence with the River Rea and Hockley Brook, the Cross-City and Walsall railway lines and Salford Junction, where the Grand Union Canal, Birmingham and Fazeley Canal and Tame Valley Canal meet.

The bulldozers made short work of the Erdington Arms, Leamington Road, Bridge Road, Woodland Road and most of Copeley Hill. The remaining houses whose uninterrupted vista across Salford Park and the lake changed forever. My school friend, a remaining resident joined the blood lead monitoring scheme.

The first two concrete motorway decking support columns were erected at the bottom of Copeley Hill, which ironically seemed to be the last part to be completed as the light concrete structure grew towards the sky and everything else left behind on the ground grew darker.

I so looked forward to its opening. The Aston Expressway with its seven lanes, flashing lights and the tidal flow system was a space age dream that would sweep away the traffic jams of Lichfield Road in an instant and convey you to, through and beyond town.

With the motorway system being bought right onto our doorstep, we could finally have a holiday with swift comfortable travel. Holiday travel down the A5 to exotic locations like Rhyl was always a nightmare.

The planners and architects were also keen to sell their baby with the self-same promise of goodies. On the new Victoria Road Island, they installed this row of benches so that joe public could sit and watch the passing Aston Expressway traffic in extreme comfort.

As you can imagine, you had to stand well clear in case you were trampled under the rush of people eager to try out this new form of entertainment.

Nobody loves a baby as much as its mother.

We call it Spaghetti Junction.

The planners call it Gravelly Hill Interchange.

We still call it Spaghetti Junction.

LANDMARKS

Gravelly Hill Interchange, Junction 6 of the M6 (haiku)

Gravelly Hill Junction
Like a can of spaghetti
Spread over the land.

Ian Henery
13/6/23

Birmingham Spaghetti Western

(After Brendan Hawthorne's "Western Spaghetti (Birthday Greetings to Gravelly Hill)")

A wave of destruction through Gravelly Hill
Down lines of canal and river network.
Pure vandalism of communities
By Birmingham planners - plandalism -
An earthquake that imprisoned people -
Gravelly Hill Interchange, Junction 6:
Landmark structure, "spaghetti junction"
Due to the intersecting traffic lanes.

There's nearly 600 concrete columns,
80 feet high over 30 acres;
18 routes split on 5 different levels
With 200,000 vehicles per day
Including 26,000 lorries.
Described by the Guinness Book of Records
"Most complex in the British roads system",
Off the grid on towers of concrete columns.

A wild spaghetti western interchange
Lacking only Clint Eastwood in the frame
To keep the cowboy sales reps and builders
In line as all the lanes rapidly change;
Cross now, lane change, closure, steel cats
   eyes glint
Their glances as arc lights illuminate
Spaghetti complexity to lasso
Cattle trucks, terror and passing strangers.

The good, the bad and ugly roam slip
   roads
Turning the air blue with constant sirens,
Concrete killing fields in the community,
Addicted to white lines and tooting horns.
Mothers with children rub their hard
   shoulders
With managing directors and teachers,
All lost in a grey tangle of tarmac,
Seeking salvation from the daily grind.

Ian Henery
13/6/23

Lord Nelson Monument

The Statue of Horatio Nelson by Richard Westmacott, RA (1775–1856) stands in the Bull Ring, Birmingham, England. This bronze statue was the first publicly funded statue in Birmingham, and the first statue of Horatio Nelson in Britain. It was made in 1809 by public subscription of £2,500 by the people of Birmingham following Nelson's visit to the town on 31 August 1802, the year before he sailed against the fleets of Napoleon. The statue was unveiled on 25 October 1809, that being the day decreed as the official golden jubilee of George III.

Nelson stands in uniform, with his one arm resting on an anchor with the prow of a miniature ship: HMS Victory. Upon the ship is the Flag Staff Truck (part of the mast) of the French ship Orient (1791), flagship of the etc, etc, etc.

Monuments have been created for thousands of years and are a type of structure that was explicitly created to commemorate a person or event, or something that has become relevant to a social group as a part of their remembrance of historic times or cultural heritage. Some monuments also serve to reinforce political power. The term monumentality relates to the symbolic status and physical presence of a monument.

Monuments have finite lives. While many are lost in time through events or accidentally destroyed along with the passage of time and the natural forces of erosion taking its toll. However, more powerful is the force of familiarity.

Familiarity with everyday indeed erodes the curiosity of the passers-by. There is nothing more invisible to the human eye than a monument. The remarkable thing about monuments is that in time one does not notice them.

It may be that some monuments are now may possibly be unable to influence the senses of the observer. It may be that our own perceptions have changed and altered, or the areas around have become more vibrant and interesting. Lord Nelson now is competing with the iconic Selfridges Store and the Bronze Bull in the Bull Ring who holds the power to pull away the casual passer-by.

Because There Is No C In Birmingham (acrostic)

(Statue of Horatio Nelson, Bullring, Birmingham)

Birmingham isn't a ship on the sea
Endeavouring to find new lands to claim;
Colonies for the British monarchy
And subjects to rule under England's name.
Understand - Britannia rules, rules the
   waves,
Sun never sets on the British Empire;
English spoken, from cradle to the grave -

But that was long ago, consumed by fire.
History teaches everything must change:
England is just an island off Europe:
Rule Britannia no more, it sounds deranged
Embarrassing - a bitter drink to sup.

Island nation, now struggling with woke,
Sleeps no more, awakens to a new age

Not yesterday under slavery's yoke -
Open your eyes to our history's books!

Captured in freeze frame, forgotten statue

It stands on a plinth, Birmingham's Bullring

Nelson - unseen by people who pass
   through

Bags in both hands, focused on their
   shopping,
Intent on social media profiles.
Rapturously they pose for their selfies,
Mesmerised by beauty, they pout and smile
At their own reflection unhealthily.
Nelson looks down on this, not of their
   world,
Gazing into screens or heading to shops.
He is trapped, no Royal Ensign is unfurled,
As unpalatable as bilge water slops
Marooned on a plinth, history's full stop.

Ian Henery
11/6/23

(The bronze statue was the first statue of Nelson in Britain. It was made in 1809 following Nelson's visit to Birmingham. Following the Rhodes Must fall campaign in South Africa and the removal of confederate monuments in the United States statutes of Nelson faced criticism because of his support for slavery and colonialism. An identical statue in Bridgetown Barbados - by the same sculpture and based on the same design - was defaced and a sign attached describing Nelson as a "racist white supremacist". The Birmingham statue includes a short biography of Nelson but doesn't mention the issues of colonialism or slavery).

Conversation with Horatio Nelson in Birmingham's Bullring

My life became painfully immobile
Following my visit to Birmingham
And sailing out to meet Napoleon.
We were expected to do our duty
And I did - the Battle of Trafalgar.
Uniformed, with HMS Victory
But now forgotten - except by pigeons -
I am just an invisible statue.

Birmingham's first public memorial,
The first of its kind in the British Isles.
Scowling bronze visage from a pedestal:
Reposed, one arm resting on an anchor,
Fenced by iron spikes, flanked by four
   cannons
Which supported magnificent lamp posts.
Now invisible? How did it happen?
A statue unnoticed in the Bullring?

I beheld surrender of the seasons,
Reminder of cultural heritage.
A monument of political power,
Physical presence, symbolic status,
I saw it all. Watched springs turn to winters,
Survived Nazi air raids, IRA bombs,
But my gnawing vacancy grew within
And into a throbbing bottomless void.

Why? I thought I was a secular saint,
Naval hero who sacrificed his life
Saving my country from Napoleon.
A painting shortly after Trafalgar
Showed me ascending to Mount Olympus
On the wings of angels to take my place
Amongst the gods - the start of an orgy
Of commemoration across Empire.

Within this bronze shell, my still beating heart,
Infected by loss and bitter anguish -
Through turning of the years - I have evolved
Into a forgotten obscure statue;
Rooted both silently and helplessly,
Watching Birmingham's diverse life flourish
Like a movie patron views from afar
The screen - but there is no happy ending.

Off the grid, rainwater on my parched tongue,
Hungry man must be fed, weeping infant
Will seek sanctuary and affection
And an exhausted body seeks out rest.
Truisms of human experience,
As is our common desire to be loved.
Am I to be mocked, held up in contempt,
For yearning for what is natural?

On my plinth in a labyrinth of shops
I have vainly sought out warmth and passion.
Under the neon lights blaring out brands,
Encircling apartments, adverts, glass
And more steel-plated walls of reflection
My sad image has withered and mocked me -
Perched in the Bullring, imperial clad -
Just a forgotten Birmingham statue.

I have not been targeted by protesters
Like those in Cape Town, Kyiv or Charlottesville,
The campaigns against imperialism.
I stand here covered in pigeon droppings,
Compete with iconic Selfridges store
And the Bronze Bull in Birmingham's Bullring
Just out of place - like colonialism -
A forgotten part of the cityscape.

I know other colonial statues,
The handsome faces of English statesmen,
Become covered in names of passers by
Or lovers with a permanent marker
And based neither on fondness nor grudges.
What's my legacy? In sight, out of mind,
Relic, put on a plinth and forgotten,
Much like our imperial legacy?

I will not succumb to imprisonment
Or modern history's woke world order.
A saviour will come, with chisel in hand
And I will be taken down and released,
Set free – to become a chameleon,
Merge unobserved into the city's heart
And, into my new lifeless surroundings
Forgotten - at one with the bricks and mortar.

Ian Henery
11/7/23

There is a statue in Birmingham's Bullring that commemorates the Battle of Trafalgar. It's the statue of an arch imperialist that once imposed a racist and violent order and it's now covered with pigeon droppings

Edgbaston Cricket Ground

I never really thought of this site as a significant landmark until recent years. It was an eclectic mix of buildings that had evolved over a number of years as the status of the cricket club has grown. It reflected a cautious approach to expansion taking one step at a time with almost a different agenda or plan at each step. It was a real Heath Robinson bits and pieces stadium that had evolved over many iterations of no particular style and no particular long term plan.

This is understandable when you take into consideration its long history. Situated on the banks of the River Rea, Edgbaston in Birmingham has been the home of Warwickshire County Cricket Club since 1885. It had a long period of just being a cricket club, seeing out two world wars. The first piece of development in the post war era was the construction of the Rea Bank and the Thwaite Memorial Scoreboard in 1950.

This big step gave the site a new status as it was then considered to be one of England's leading cricket grounds right after Lord's. This newfound status trigged a chain of other developments. In 1956 an Indoor Cricket School was built, and the Pavilion Suite was completed in the same year. In 1967 the William Ansell Stand opened to cheers and hoorays. Executive boxes were added in 1989 before the capacity of the ground was increased to 17,500.

Edgbaston has hosted some notable international matches. The final match of the first Women's Cricket World Cup was played here in 1973. It was also the venue for a thrilling match in the 2005 Ashes, considered one of the best of all time. It saw England win by 2 runs (England's narrowest Test victory in terms of runs). It hosted the first senior game under floodlights in English cricket in July 1997 between Warwickshire and Somerset in the then AXA Life Sunday League and the first day/night Test match in England in August 2017 when England played the West Indies.

More recently, the Pavilion end underwent a makeover in 2010 at a cost of £32 million which saw the capacity of the ground rise to 25,000. Five permanent floodlights were also installed in 2011 to allow 15 days of day-night cricket annually. The first test to be played at the ground following the development was England vs India, which saw England rise to the number one ranking in the ICC Test Championship. However, this is only one of a number of notable moments that have occurred on the hallowed turf at Edgbaston.

These most recent developments have given Edgbaston a true identity of its own. It is now a mixed-use destination with cricket and community at its core, realising the legacy of the 2022 Commonwealth Games in Birmingham. It combines elite sport, conferencing and events with community assets aimed at improving health and social care, education, employment, and social cohesion in the area. The iconic design has a striking bright blue clad exterior with full height glass panel windows which give it a distinctive presence and with its 'e' (for Edgbaston) flood lighting it now proudly holds the status of a landmark.

Edgbaston Cricket Ground (haiku)

Ball thrown at wickets
Slap of leather on willow
It's just not cricket

Ian Henery
12/6/23

Holy Trinity Church

Holy Trinity Church, Camp Hill, Bordesley, Birmingham once stood head and shoulders above the surrounding area in an ever changing Birmingham. It is a is a Grade II listed former Church of England parish church built between 1820 and 1822 by the architect Francis Goodwin. The church is said to have been modelled on King's College Chapel, Cambridge. The light honey coloured Bath Stone used in its construction gives it a very distinctive appearance, noticeable for miles.

It was once the site of the most important Anglo-Catholic controversies in Birmingham and was the centre of a simmering row over high church practices introduced by vicar Richard William Enraght. His trial in 1880, dubbed the Bordesley Wafer Case, gripped the nation. He advocated "ritualism" – a blend of Catholic and C of E practices, and was prosecuted for using eucharist candles, wafer bread in Holy Communion and allowing Agnus Dei to be sung – all forbidden by the bishop. Father Enraght refused to attend his own trial, brought under the Public Worship Regulation Act, and received the maximum penalty – imprisonment and dismissal from the parish.

It ceased being a place of worship in 1971 just at the time I became an apprentice attending Christ Church School of Art and Decorating in Sparkbrook. An annex of Birmingham Polytechnic Collage. As a 16 year old, it seemed quite a long bus ride from Erdington through town and beyond into an area previously unknown. Holy Trinity Church was like a milestone, indicating a significant part of the journey was complete and I was on course and heading in the right direction.

There were plans afoot to turn it into Trinity Arts Centre, but this only ever got as far as a graffiti sign on the doors indicating an aspiration never fulfilled. For many years it served as Trinity Night shelter for the homeless, and today it currently stands empty.

As I looked at the church to take these photos, it appeared lonely and forlorn on the top of Old Camp Hill. Now isolated in a virtual traffic island between the roundabouts known as Bordesley Circus and Camp Hill Circus on the Middleway Ring Road, it's a landmark that has become invisible in the landscape, familiarity eroding away the curiosity of the casual passer-by.

I see this object and it evokes fond memories of a youthful past. It was a place I could use to orientate myself in an unfamiliar area when out of my comfort zone. Now I love this area and feel both happy and at ease whenever I walk here.

Holy Trinity Church, Camphill (haiku)

For sale - gothic church
Just be careful of gravestones
Boast rooms with a pew.

Ian Henery
14/6/23

The 203 year old church is up for sale and comes complete with an 83 foot spire and congregational capacity for 1,821 people - ideal for larger families

Birthplace of Birmingham City Football Club

(Holy Trinity Church) (haiku)

Players in the choir
Football is a religion
Birthplace of the Blues.

Ian Henery
14/6/23

True worshippers at St Andrews will know that the Blues began at Holy Trinity Church when members of the choir formed a cricket team in 1871. To keep fit over the winter the cricketers decided to try the new sport of Association Football and, in 1875, became known as Small Heath Alliance Football Club. In 1888 they were renamed Small Heath and, in 1943, Birmingham City.

EDGES

Moseley Golf Course

An Impenetrable Division

Moseley Golf Club was founded in 1892 and boasts a superb parkland course designed by the renowned Harry Colt. It is a challenging but fair test for golfers of all abilities with immaculate greens in use throughout the year.

The 106 acre course is surrounded by an impenetrable 3 kilometre boundary with 1.7 kilometres of fencing fronting the surrounding roads building a continuous form. The remainder is enclosed by housing that has developed since the course's inception.

The golf club has gone to an immense effort to keep access impenetrable to both to the unwelcome guest, the curious passer-by, or anyone else wishing to look and enjoy the parkland.

Copious amounts of chain-link, closeboard fencing with padlocked gates and barbed wire reinforce the desire of the club to keep all onlookers out, with of course the exception of members.

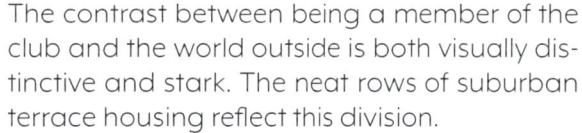

The contrast between being a member of the club and the world outside is both visually distinctive and stark. The neat rows of suburban terrace housing reflect this division.

Moseley Golf Course (haiku)

   Superb parkland course
   Ensconced in barb wire and chain
   For members - of course.

Ian Henery
20/11/23

Moseley Golf Club

The anticipated digital photographs came
                              WeTransfer
Edges of Moseley Golf Club,
Clearly defined boundaries,
Continuous and impenetrable.

The poet tries to write a poem
                            about golfers
Comically dressed in overpriced clothes,
Hitting little white balls
With big expensive sticks

And talking about it for hours
                            in hallowed parkland
Free from the stares
Of the great unwashed proletariat,
Ensconced behind their high fences.

The poet tries to write a poem
                            saw the metaphor
Current immigration policies -
Chain fences and barbed wire,
Refugees locked out of England's green and
   pleasant land.

The poet tries to write a poem
                            terraced housing
Lined up outside the parkland,
Foaming like a roaring tsunami
Held back by a strip of road.

The poet tries to write a poem
                            about edges.
Was the fencing to keep out undesirables
Or the precious ones caged in?
Pure specimens free from contagion,
Working class plebs like the poet?
                            No poem written
About the immaculate greens,
A superb parkland course,
Off the grid - members only.

Ian Henery
22/11/23

NODES

Birmingham Bullring

The Bullring in Birmingham is almost as old as the city itself, the market having played a central role in the development of the city from the 12th century right through to the present day. Its marketing activity has made it a natural focus point where roads and paths converge to give the perception of a centre of Birmingham.

This central point has brought thousands of people together for centuries. Traders, artisans, travellers, and local people from all across the world came here giving Birmingham the title "City of a Thousand Trades".

Since the Middle Ages the centre of Birmingham has been subject to constant change, with new buildings gradually replacing their predecessors. The iconic Bullring, however, has transcended time.

Allegedly a place where the practice of bull-baiting took place, it is still unclear whether the name originally referred to the area or to the ring to which the bull was tethered. The site now has a very clear identity of its own. A monument to Birmingham in its own right.

Because of this long history of constant change, this is a monument that has not become invisible as many others have due to their familiarity to the casual passerby. It has rewritten its own identity to remain in tune with the everyday people of Birmingham and stands head and shoulders strong and resilient like a bull.

The bull is now a meeting place in the city and its symbolic meaning has changed over time. The use of the bull in the opening ceremony of the commonwealth games illustrates this. The bull, like the everyday working people of the city had, in the past, been misused and abused. Bulls were ill-treated in the bullring as were everyday people who worked in the sweatshops of the industrial Midlands.

Released from the shackles of oppression, the bull, like its people, is now a symbol of reconciliation, peace, and happiness showcasing Birmingham's cultural richness in a setting of civility and conviviality in the 'super-diverse' context of Birmingham.

What is not to love?

Bull in the Bullring (villanelle)

The bull is now a meeting place for all
No longer a symbol of oppression
A landmark in Birmingham's shopping halls.

Commonwealth Games, an armoured bull enthralled
Female chain makers, free from repression;
The bull is now a meeting place for all.

Workers free from chains, tyranny's downfall,
Bulls baited in bullrings by aggression
A landmark in Birmingham's shopping halls.

Released from sweatshops in this urban sprawl
Chains and bondage broken through expression
The bull is now a meeting place for all.

Working people, retail therapy trawl,
Not misused and abused by suppression
A landmark in Birmingham's shopping halls.

Bulls in Bullring and train station installed,
Chained bulls are baited no more, progression;
The bull is now a meeting place for all
A landmark in Birmingham's shopping halls.

16/12/23
Ian Henery

Released from the Shackles of Oppression (Bull in the Bullring)

Symbolic meaning has changed
Bulls baited in the Bullring
And everyday people in sweatshops.
Industrial Revolution, bondage and chains
Opening ceremony, Commonwealth
  Games.
Bulls baited and everyday people
In sweatshops in the Bullring.
Industrial Revolution, Commonwealth
  Games
Opening ceremony, bondage and chains
Symbolic meaning has changed.

16/12/23
Ian Henery

After Cicely Herbert's "Everything Changes" - Poems on the Underground.

DISTRICTS

Short Heath – New Utopia

The aftermath of World War I saw cultural, economic, and social change across the world. Empires collapsed, some countries were abolished, and new ones created. Maps and boundaries were redrawn. National organisations were abolished, and international organisations were established. While Germany was humiliated and burdened with war reparations, Britain was crippled psychologically, but economically it fared well, and many new ideologies took a firm hold in people's minds. It was during this period that housing policy became explicitly political. In the cities, local parties competed with each other to promise more and more homes, while in Westminster, worried ministers saw a programme of housebuilding as an essential bulwark against the tide of revolution sweeping other parts of Europe. As the Secretary to the Local Government Board put it: 'The money we are going to spend on housing is an insurance against Bolshevism and Revolution.'

The social housing in the Short Heath area of Birmingham is part of the first flush of post-World War I idealism. Under the 1919 Housing Act, the long term vision was to create a municipal dream, a new utopia.

To fulfil the dream of a new utopia, basic needs had to be met. Birmingham Council's Housing Direct Labour Department embarked on one of the biggest house building programmes in Europe, starting in the Short Heath Area. The homes were basic three bedroomed semi and terraced houses with a kitchen, bathroom, a living room, coal store and an outside toilet. A little over ten per cent of homes had a parlour too. The design was based around the living style of the time, architectural niceties took a back seat with a five door kitchen. For warmth there was a coal fire or cooking range. Most houses did not have a hot water system, the bath filled from the wash boiler.

Ample gardens provided space for the tenants to grow their own food with additional provision in the form of allotment gardens. Nearby park space provided opportunities for leisure.

The vision of a world class road infrastructure shaped the layout of the estates. The plan of wide duel carriageways with trams running on the central reservation, cycle lanes between the road and wide grass verges, and ample pavements positioned the building line for future growth.

High on the list of priorities were health and well-being. Purpose-built Welfare Centres sprang up in convenient places where vitamin tablets, cod-liver oil, orange juice and national dried milk would be issued along with vaccinations for polio etc.

With an increasing and more healthy working population growth was inevitable. The growing educational needs were met by the construction of new schools and extensions of existing sites. A culture of air and light formed the basis of school design with rows of classrooms having opening doors down both sides to let in air and high windows to let in light.

With a shortage of men following WWI, skilled employment was at a premium. Birmingham being an industrialised town and men being seen as the bead winners the brewing industry saw an opportunity to extract cash from working men. Positioned on major road junctions and near bus routes a number of substantially large pubs were built with multiple rooms and bars for the working man to indulge. These places were geared up to extract as much money as possible from working men before they had been home with their wages.

This new utopia seems an ideal lifestyle. Homes for working class people with amenities for heath and leisure, transport and education. It was a time of improving equality and a glowing bright future. However, in Germany war reparations were causing inflation and poverty. Inequality was rife. A new political landscape was emerging. The Nazi Party held the most seats in the German Reichstag and Hitler became chancellor then head of state and of the German Government. His aggressive foreign policy gave all of the indications that Britain should prepare for war. New changes appeared in the landscape including air raid shelters and other markings for the preparation for war.

On 1 September 1939, Germany invaded Poland, and the rest of the world held its breath.

Post World War One Idealism – A Municipal Dream

A New Utopia

Everything changes
The snowdrops die, daisies carpet the lawn
Punctuated by sunny buttercups.
Off the grid, bats and hedgehogs
Patrol suburban gardens.

The snowdrops die, bats and hedgehogs
Patrol suburban gardens.
Daisies carpet the lawn
Punctuated by sunny buttercups
Off the grid, everything changes.

Ian Henery
30/5/23

After Cicely Herbert's "Everything Changes" – *Poems on the Underground*.

Sonnet To Slightly Bruised Fruit

Slightly bruised fruit on the allotment shelf
And my gorgeous flesh is no longer firm:
One of your 5-a-day to make you squirm,
Fruit and vegetables are good for your health.
In the allotment I was gardeners' wealth
But now no longer perfect and cast out;
Ego is bruised, off the grid, here I pout,
My good looks have been stolen by Time's stealth.

I'm just slightly bruised! I still taste the same!
Is it my fault I was dropped on the floor?
An endless fumbling in sweaty paws?
I blossomed, grew, witnessed summer's flame,
Birds sang in my tree, knew them all by name.
I'm at one with the air, the sky and earth.
Just slightly bruised – how can I have no worth?
What is my crime and how am I to blame?

Ian Henery
30/5/23

Allegory for social inclusion - we all have issues. You wouldn't throw your legs away if your knees got bruised, would you?

DISTRICTS

The Little Path

The little path, half lost beneath the woods,
Runs on the hillside where, in some old days,
Strange shapes of men moved at their task of life
As me, who trod this path, move still and gaze
Across Short Heath, blue with summer haze.

Plain where the trees fall towards the midday sun
The path winds on above the heathland scar
And, off the grid against a pale blue sky,
Turns from our sight – but on the upland afar –
Passes where the deepest strobes of green shadows are

And beneath the hawthorn woods that stand listening
In Maytime's peace in repose, save where, dry
About our feet Autumn's leaves rustle, runs
The little path. Afternoon closes and with a sigh
Day's banners tumble from the stricken sky.

The years in long procession come and go;
The warm gold summers and the autumn rain,
With smiles and tears, go by the fields and woods
Where we passed once and may not pass again
Though still our footsteps in the grass remain.

Sleep lightly in the weight of time, Birmingham,
That made me glad; and when the darkening vale
Lies deep in dusk's embrace and from the sky
The last sun, smothering fires of daylight fail
On Short Heath's hill the little path glimmers pale

Though I, in passing, shall not stir the dew
Though sweet years of nostalgia will meet in that still heart
Of Birmingham. The night, voiceless and calm,
Will quiver with the words that may not start
From memories the passage of time cannot part.

Ian Henery
30/5/23

(In the style of A.E. Housman)

Suburban Dawn (After Brendan Hawthorne's "Urban Dawn")

The red scar sunrise
Glides through cold, steel skies
And high pressure sodium street lights
Fade their saintly blue halos
Over roadways and ring roads.

Electric light melt into furnace-orange doorways,
Another suburban dawn in Birmingham.
Short Heath awakens and, off the grid,
Witnesses the triumphal entrance -
The birth of light

Before the fires of day seize
Parked cars revving in anticipation
Of somewhere else to go:
Commuters to warehouses, offices or factories
Amongst a landscape of central reservations

Dual carriageways and grass verges.
Warmth given to school children at bus stops,
Gardeners in allotments, dog walkers, joggers in the park.
All blissfully illuminated
In this new utopia of a municipal dream.

Ian Henery
30/5/23

"The social housing in the Short Heath area of Birmingham is part of the first flush of post-World war 1 idealism. Under the 1919 Housing Act, the long term vision was to create a municipal dream, a new utopia. As the Secretary to the Local Government Board put it: 'The money we are going to spend on housing is an insurance against Bolshevism and Revolution'." - David Moore

The Lisieux Trust in Marsh Lane (villanelle)

(NeurodiVERSE)

"Autism didn't stop Einstein, Mozart, Newton or Temple Grandin reaching the stars!"

Support those with a disability
We provide accommodation and care,
We just have different abilities.

Happy lives full of opportunity,
Create independence, choice and health care
Support those with a disability.

Skills needed to thrive in society,
Special needs, off the grid, "here" not "nowhere":
We just have different abilities.

All of our people have nobility,
We nurture their confidence and welfare,
Support those with a disability.

Tenancy and responsibility,
Supported living and not "anywhere";
We just have different abilities.

We're blessed with powers of capability,
Our people are the answers to our prayer:
Support those with a disability,
We just have different abilities.

Ian Henery
31/5/23

(More information about the Lisieux Trust: http://www.lisieuxtrust.org.uk.)

This poem is written in the form of a Villanelle. "The building was originally a Welfare Centre where vitamin tablets, cod liver oil, orange juice and dried milk would be issued along with vaccinations for polio."
- David Moore who attended the Welfare Centre as a child.

Court Farm Primary School (rondeau) ("Dream, Believe, Achieve")

Our Court Farm School, dare to believe
Success and the power to achieve;
In teamwork and community for all,
Continued learning when we all leave.

Motivated children in sleeves
And through education they weave,
Future leaders in children small
Our Court Farm School

Off the grid, to our motto cleave
As through life like a cannon ball:
Keep memories from playground to hall
The motto "Dream, Believe, Achieve"
Our Court Farm School.

Ian Henery

31/5/23

This poem is written in the form of a rondeau. David Moore went to this school as a child. "New schools after the war saw a culture of air and light with rows of classrooms having opening doors down both sides to let in light and air and high windows to let in light" - David Moore.

Conversation In A Pub (Apologies to Tom Waits and the 1973 album *Closing Time*)

Well, I hope I don't fall in love with you
Sitting alone, do you need company?
This old tom cat soul could never be true.
Have you come in here to forget, like me?
Do you have time for the tears of a clown
And humour me as all my troubles drown?

Well, I hope I don't fall in love with you,
I don't want to corrupt you with my heart;
It's always searching for someone new,
Perhaps it's better we should be apart.
There must be a more worthy man in town
Off the grid under evening's ragged gown.

Well, I hope I don't fall in love with you,
Emotional attention is a curse;
If we do go to bed, this night you'll rue,
Charity to have listened to this in verse.
I am but a tumbleweed ever blown,
It's a job description in verb and noun.

Well, I hope I don't fall in love with you -
It's last orders, I hear the barmaid shout.
Let's have another beer, I've drunk a few;
What you drinking? I'm having Irish stout.
If such sad acts were king, I'd wear a crown;
Depressed? No! See this smile? I'm never down.

Well, I hope I don't fall in love with you -
Don't want to annoy you with words that rhyme.
Last orders but you've gone - my feelings grew
In the pub's tick of my borrowed time.
You see I love you but I'm just a clown
And you've gone - so in tears and beer I'll drown.

31/5/23
Ian Henery

"After the war men were seen as the breadwinners. The brewing industry saw an opportunity to extract cash from working men. Positioned on major road junctions and near bus routes a number of substantially large pubs were built with multiple rooms and bars for the working man to indulge. These places were geared up to extract as much money as possible from working men before they had been home with their wages." – David Moore

Remains of Tram Lines on a Central Reservation

Here lie the remains of utopia,
New social housing and idealism,
Creation of a municipal dream
After war and years of dystopia.

War to end all wars - Europe redrawn
Cultural and social change across the world
And new housing needed in Birmingham
To fulfil the dream in the post war dawn.

Tram lines on a central reservation
Traces of ages-lost idealism;
Archaeological evidence unearthed,
Fear of Bolshevism and Revolution.

Here, where waves of grass and the earth
   worms creep,
Where all the tides of life have ebbed and
   left;
Off the grid, the gaunt ribs of Birmingham
The men who made her mighty workers
   sleep.

And we, with equal gaze, are dumb before
The shattered stone that bears
   Birmingham's name;
The massive columns, deep in ruin, laid,
Or print of workers' boots that walk no more

Nor have walked since unnumbered suns
   have set,
The roads that lie over the barley fields.
No lore of books shall make these sleepers
   stir
But remembering them, never forget.

The glory that a thousand volumes fills,
Slumbers on a central reservation
In a vision of road infrastructure
Crafted by working class labour and skill.

Ian Henery
1/6/23

"This new utopia seems an ideal lifestyle. Homes for working class people with amenities for health and leisure, transport and education. It was a time of improving equality and a glowing bright future".
- David Moore

Thick as a Brick
(Apologies to Jethro Tull and the 1972 album *Thick as a Brick*)

Spinning back down the years
To the days of my youth
Alone, listening to Jethro Tull
"Thick as a Brick"
And drinking London dry gin.

The early hours
And another bottle of alcohol:
Comforter, maternal teat,
Sandcastle virtues all swept away
In tidal destruction.

Night. Locked out of the house,
A labourer and now sacked,
Off the grid, huddled for warmth
Amongst lawnmowers
In the garden shed.

Wise men don't know
How it feels
To be thick as a brick,
Spinning down the long ages
To sing the songs.

Pronounced fit to fight,
Told to get a job,
Taught to play Monopoly
At the kitchen table
But not to sing in the rain.

Is it really 40 years
Since that night?
Climbing into rich people's gardens,
Feeding London dry gin
To wide-eyed goldfish.

Built sandcastles by the sea,
Dared the tardy tide
To wash them away
But wise men don't know
How it feels to be thick as a brick.

Ian Henery
1/6/23

(*Thick as a Brick* by British rock band Jethro Tull is intended to be a parody of the concept album genre. The original packaging, designed as a 12-page newspaper, claims to be a musical adaptation of an epic poem by fictional 8-year old genius Gerald Bostock, although it was actually written by Ian Anderson from the band. The personal story of working as a labourer, getting sacked and sleeping in a shed are true.

Short Heath Graffiti (one last time)
(After Brendan Hawthorne's "Silent Shouting")

The stylised tag of youth culture,
Marked out turf in an act of boredom
Or to stage out a nocturnal conquest.
Graffiti continues to spell out "decay"
Off the grid while paint fades.
The message is nothing lasts forever
As the old man remembers and looks on,
Remembering youth from his memory.
Once upon a time, a new municipal dream,
An era of social housing and urban utopia.

These indifferent bricks may have forgotten him
But he remembers this wall of brick -
Can't forget -
Or that breathless kiss one magical night.
Leaning back they had watched the stars

Across the night sky of Birmingham,
Cast adrift in Short Heath
Like two marooned lovers on an island.
They etched their hearts, whispered their words
But never married

And now she's dead.
This wall is a memorial to their love,
Testimony to their acts of passion
And the old man, full of regret, cries:
Someone has spray-painted a stupid tag

Across the wall where love was found -
His wall - their wall - and he wishes
He could trace her name
Just one last time
Over these bricks.

Ian Henery
1/6/23

PATHS

Moseley Road - a Journey from Victorian Inequality to a Wealth of Cultural Diversity.

Looking at Moseley Road.

The Guru Nanak Gurduwara Bhay Singh Sabah and Community Centre.

Mosley Road Library and Baths.

Mosely Road was originally a Turnpike Road. I have this imaginary image of a grand toll house and gates. Certainly, the houses are reflective of the wealth generated from the industrial city of a thousand trades. It was a gilded age; for some.

The architecture of these grand houses makes a bold statement of prosperous wealth and success. The fine lines and tall windows letting light and air into well-appointed drawing rooms, lounges, and studies. However, how happy these nouveaux riches were is debatable. While they claim to have done alright for themselves, their need of wanting something bigger, better, grander with power over others is rarely synonymous with happiness.

The architecture of this house also makes a hidden statement about poverty and inequality. The tiny window on the top left is almost an afterthought. More to do with architectural symmetry than functioning well lit rooms for domestic staff. Indeed, the domestic staff lived in a very different world.

Mosley Road was cut, intersected by a bypass that's now an extension of Alcester Road to Camp Hill, the grand turnpike road now relegated to the second division of side road status.

The Quakers Friends' Institute was once a fine building that fell into disuse in the late 60's. Ironically, with inequality on the rise again it has found a new use as a community advice centre and food bank. The site is run by people who have done all right for themselves and have come together to do all right for others. It is these projects that make me happy. I am pleased to be associated with these remarkable individuals who have built a rich and diverse community.

It was near here I met the road sweeper. He was an incredibly happy guy. He told me how he was doing a worthwhile job and serving the community to help others. I am now a richer individual for meeting and spending time with this guy.

The width of the road is a past remnant of the aspirations of the road designers. The Victorians seem to have had grand plans at attempting to future proof their endeavours. This gilded age came to an end following two terrible world wars, with the population looking for a fresh start. A lot of older buildings had to make way for new developments built to meet the changing needs of a changing population. The Guru Nanak Gurduwara Bhay Singh Sabah and Community Centre is one such place. The sense of identity carefully placed on the dome, the signage and the gates makes a statement about this cultural change.

At the end of Moseley Road, we look on from afar at the Baths and Library. When originally opened at the turn of the twentieth century, these establishment would have been out of reach of the everyday working person. Now with the changes they have moved in time and place from Victorian Inequality to a Wealth of Cultural Diversity.

Moseley Road (found poem) (Apologies to Ocean Colour Scene)

Do you recall the day we caught the train?
Two of us, singing The Riverboat Song;
Off the grid, in Moseley Shoals, in the rain?
Moseley Village vibes, we knew we belonged:
40 past midnight and one for the road,
Policemen and pirates, where the river flowed.

You sang "Where is the love? Where is the soul?"
The river turned to tarmac and was dead;
Dreams were ground with litter in Moseley Shoals,
You've got it bad, the downstream up ahead
And like a king you stalked up Moseley Road,
Time to get away where the river flowed.

30 years later and my fleeting mind
Lining your pockets, photographs you took;
Life is like a circle, time to rewind:
It's my shadow, I come again to look -
You stalking like a king up Moseley Road
And singing your songs where the river flowed.

Ian Henery
26/2/2023

This poem took inspiration from the lyrics of The Riverboat Song by Moseley band Ocean Colour Scene. The titles of every song from Moseley Shoals appear in this poem.

The Old House (Ferndale House, Moseley Road)

When I return, off the grid and a ghost,
No former tenement will know my tread;
But where the spring-time blossom's raiments spread
Their rich brocade I'll wear.

The old house - a place my heart loves the most
Sheltered under a cathedral of trees;
It's a gloom of green as translucent seas
A peace beyond compare.

Together again from the spirit host
Silently we'll gather in Moseley Road,
Pass under the trees where the blossoms snowed
Unseen, no one to stare.

Ian Henery
26/2/23

Thumbs Up To A Road Sweeper On Moseley Road

Thumbs up!
Got a trolley with all my tools,
Free as a bird, make my own rules;
Kitted out in hi-vis and gloves
Off the grid and a job I love
Thumbs up!

Thumbs up!
I see no inequality
On the road but diversity.
If asked I'd say my job is skilled,
A happy man of my own will
Thumbs up!

Thumbs up!
A worthwhile job to help others -
We're one - all sisters and brothers.
Urban happiness in my work,
An important job, no time to shirk
Thumbs up!

Ian Henery
27/2/23

Night on Moseley Road Waiting For The Foodbank To Open (Quakers Friends' Institute)

After "The Way We Were" by Barbara Streisand)

"Memories"
The two women coughed their lungs out of their throats
Disembodied in cardboard and dirty coats.
Squatting in a doorway like litter on the street,
As the wind blew around decaying concrete.
Victorian streets pointing to the city,
The retch of despair heaved with anonymity
Under buildings on which transience is written,
Passing memories fade, without root and smitten.

"Like the smiles we left behind"
The hour grows late and dumped across the pavement
Fast food cartons, plastic bottles, night time scents
Splashed across the footpath or up graffitied walls
Drunken revellers, which taint and flavour all.
Work for the road sweeper - fag butts, empty cans
And chip paper beneath cars and white vans.
The two women hide within their own cocoon,
Concealed by cardboard and clouds over the moon.

"That we gave to one another"
The women pass the night with songs and yawning,
Foodbank opens 11 in the morning.
There's lots of homeless and it's limited stock
So they need to get in and don't have a clock.
Second hand clothes are 50p on the rack,
What they are wearing is soiled and look like sacks.
Now off the grid with memories and regret,
So they sang their songs so they would not forget.

"The way we were"
Homeless women, together, now all alone;
Cast off, unwanted, like fast food chicken bones.
The women sang they would do it all again,
Dreams are not litter, cast offs, left to remain.
When the sun rises the road sweeper will come,
The traffic will roar and Moseley Road will hum
But they will be gone - to the welcome foodbank -
It's here, limited stock, good people to thank.

Ian Henery
27/2/2023

A Cup of Tea At The Foodbank (Quakers Friends' Institute)

The world to whom Charlie Chaplin once performed
Comic character, in the face of cultural norms,
Romanticized the homeless through media hype
Divorced from reality as an American stereotype.
In Moseley's destitute are no dented bowlers,
None carry spotted bandanas over their shoulders:
Only a struggle with mental health and once-held dignity
Off the grid and a desperate grasp on their former identity.

Spat at, kicked and abused by those with no humanity,
Such expressions of "concern" are displayed by society.
Pathological deviants in need of strict control:
A little self-discipline is good for the soul.
Dismissed as vexatious and so they are punished,
Living out of litterbins, labelled as "rubbish".
The cutting look of eyes filled with pity or disdain:
The world soon forgets but the scars remain.

Hiding in car parks that stink of human excrement;
Sleeping in doorways with the acrid smell of disinfectant.
Drunken flung arms, staring eyes and twisted feet
Littering Birmingham, its suburbs, parks and streets.
Wandering between foodbanks in apathetic dejection,
The cheapest alcohol cushioning the blows of rejection.
Time rolls on, but its passing does not end their pain:
The world soon forgets but their agony remains.

Roaring over his cup of tea in the foodbank canteen
"It was picking up trash this place came into being!
Trash is what we are, we have no education;
We are trash on the streets of the nation!
We are fed trash and we are treated like trash,
Begging in door ways for dog ends or cash.
I am trash and trash is what we all are!
My wounds have healed but I have got my scars".

The homeless are not unwanted cast offs left behind;
We label them into pigeon holes of the mind
But they are people, not cast offs, lying in crumpled ruin
To be consigned as litter and over Moseley Village to be strewn.
The homeless need more than clean socks every week;
They are human, not litter, under society's feet:
Inequality exists within our neighbourhood,
And respect helps them more than pity ever could.

Ian Henery
28/2/23

The Khanda on Moseley Road

The Khanda
Pinned proudly on the gates for all to see,
An emblem of cultural diversity.
A holy sign of the Sikh faith and code,
Punjabi heritage to Moseley Road
The Khanda.

The Khanda
A double-edged sword, a chakram, two knives
Called "kirpan" with one God to rule their lives.
Three weapons and a circle, their belief
In Khalsa and Langar for poor relief
The Khanda.

The Khanda
Sign of God without beginning or end
A circle, duty to not just friends
But for all - in oneness - with God's love
From Moseley food banks to Heaven above
The Khanda.

The Khanda
Off the grid - a cauldron and martial might,
Food for the hungry, doing what is right;
Langar for all in the community
Regardless of the ethnicity
The Khanda.

Ian Henery
28/2/23

The Khanda is the amalgamation of 3 symbols - a double-edged sword, a chakram and two kirpan which represents Miri Piri - spiritual and temporal authority - the Sikh doctrine of providing food and protection for the needy and oppressed.

Balsall Heath Library & Moseley Road Baths

Edwardian community hub
Made of red brick and terracotta
And off the grid
Because when first built
Everyday people worked 7 days
12 to 14 hours a day
With one day off
For Christmas.
It would take a world war
To bring the baths and library
Into the grasp
Of everyday people.

Community is not just a word:
We need other people
To interact with and love:
It's what makes us truly human.
Now, more than ever,
We need strong, supportive communities.
Moseley Road in Birmingham
In search of urban happiness,
Victorian inequality to cultural diversity
And one of only 3 baths
In the entire country
Listed as Grade 2*.

Landmark of community
Library run by Birmingham City Council
And it has a clock tower:
Family friendly, computer access,
Benefit verification service,
Exhibition space, free for all.
The baths were threatened with closure,
Rescued by Friends of Moseley Road Baths,
Non- profit community enterprise.
Beautiful building, long- term future,
Well-loved and well-used,
Huge historical and architectural
   significance.

Ian Henery
2/3/23

www.ingramcontent.com/pod-product-compliance
Lightning Source LLC
Chambersburg PA
CBRC101356070526
44584CB00010B/338